A LIGHT-HEARTED LOOK AT MAN THE SOCIAL ANIMAL [NEW EDITION]

KERWIN MATHEW

A LIGHT-HEARTED LOOK AT MAN THE SOCIAL
ANIMAL [NEW EDITION]

PREFACE

No man is an island. No matter how anti-social a person may be, he cannot avoid his fellow-men. He might wish to be a hermit and could even live a hermit's life. But it is unlikely that he would be able to sustain himself as a hermit for long.

Man has physical needs - food, clothing, shelter, comfort and emotional needs such as friendship, companionship and love. However, in his attempts at satisfying his needs, man has come to be dependent on his fellow-men. In a modern society like ours, the level of technology is high and specialization is necessary. It is necessary today for each man to perform at his best and exchange their fruits of labor with each other.

It is often the case now that man has become selfish in his motives and actions. He has become a calculative creature with many wants. He has become less tolerant of others. He has become more competitive and more ruthless in action.

The author's intention through this book is to show the various psychological aspects of man. The author does not deny that this book is provocative, even controversial. Hopefully, it would "wake up ideas" and get people to act and behave properly and become better persons.

The author guides the reader through a light-hearted and yet serious review of man and his personality. To add to the excitement there is a dash of humor. This book should be able to act as a stimulus and guide by providing important insights.

The most important point is attitude. Everyone should adopt

the right attitude towards life. The author hopes that this book will help inculcate this in the reader. Hopefully, the book will help the reader grow wiser and become better at relating with his fellow-beings.

Kerwin Mathew, Ph.D.

CONTENTS

1 INTRODUCTION

"We've not really understood our inner self, our mind, what's the point of trying to understand all things exterior?" - Anonymous

There is the almost magical gift, the mind, the quality of which makes one a successful person, a failure, or a mediocrity. The qualities of the mind are measured in relative terms such as brightness, melancholy or cheerfulness. No one is bright if there are no mediocrities and no fools. The reader should be able to control the workings of his own mind if he understands how the mind works.

The most important factor governing our life is happiness. Our mind is constantly seeking this happiness, and even seeks it through God, through religion. Therefore, it could be said that the mind was born for happiness and to seek happiness. The factors that rob our happiness, such as misfortunes and failures, make us melancholic, anxious or depressed. Undoubtedly, a little bit of anxiety or sorrow now and again is normal in life, but too much of it is abnormal and deprives us of our happiness, for anxiety or sorrow in excess is a worry in itself for its ill and harmful effects to health, both mental and physical.

Man goes through life with a certain goal, e.g., to achieve success in a career and to settle down. Some may want to influence society and be its head and some may seek to help the underprivileged throughout their lifetime. Without these goals, man would not know how to live or why he must live. A man wants to be helpful because he believes in impressing people and he would feel a certain satisfaction in doing so, a satisfaction that results from the elevation of the self.

Without goals to occupy or pre-occupy the mind, man would behave without consideration, without discretion, and in a more Machiavellian manner.

The mind is responsible for the rise as well as downfall of man. From simple cave-dwellers, we have progressed to complex individuals, using complex machines and equipment. It is the mind which makes the inventions and the discoveries. An inventor may understand the working of a complex machinery, a mathematician or a physicist may pride himself on his discoveries. If these people have but little understanding about the mechanism of the mind, then they have missed a great deal in their life. Intellectuals should have a great understanding of the mind and should know their standing in society. Attitude is also responsible for advancement. For progress and advancement, it is important to be able to choose the right attitude to adopt and to have the confidence and the courage to choose the right course of action when the opportunity occurs.

Therefore, to try to understand the mind fully is one of the requisites for a happy life. Often to try to understand others, we have to put ourselves in their positions and try to analyze the problems they would be facing. We should also try to analyze ourselves and our problems. All this may be a time-consuming process. However, we should try to understand a fellow-man's general behavior, e.g., why a person talks excessively, why he keeps quiet, and why he is restless, broods and feels moody. You can probably explain this excessive talkativeness as an escape from an anxious, moody feeling. Similarly, other behaviors can also be explained after careful analysis of a person's mental frame.

To understand the mind, to let reason predominate over emotion, i.e., in one's relationship with others one should exercise one's power of reason, is a highly important state of affair. Many a time, a person may lose control of his power of reason, especially in affairs concerning himself, e.g., a person may make wrong decisions concerning himself. But he who is constantly aware of the fact that he has done something unreasonable and feels bad about it, or he who always feels proud or happy that he has done something in line with reason, he is the wise man, the man with great intellectual potential, the man worth admiring.

A person thinks best when he is writing, and he can link his ideas up in writing and is able to create more and more original ideas; thinking can only be well organized when one is writing about one's ideas. George Bernard Shaw had prided himself on thinking twice a week; while writing, he probably produced his best thoughts, and writing probably gave him the meaning in thinking. Shaw was proud of thinking a great deal and said other people hardly thought more than a few times throughout the year. Thinking has little meaning if it is merely a reflection of the mind. Thinking should materialize in words which would be read or listened to and which should be appreciated and educate; only then can thinking have much meaning as they can bear the tangible fruits of its labor. It is little use keeping the ideas to oneself; it may be better to pass them to others, to use them to improve others or to use them to improve oneself.

It is futile to be to be intellectual, if others do not appreciate your intellect; you are then no better than a fool whose intellect also lacks appreciation. Pleasing and influencing others with his intellect should be the ultimate purpose of the intellectual.

The analysis of the mind is important as the mind is mysterious; it is capable of revealing its nature that is mainly consciousness with another aspect of life in the unconscious part, the unconscious mind. The unconscious mind which is responsible for our desires and our fears and which is all the more mystifying in that it plays tricks in the form of dreams or sleep-walks and would reveal itself under hypnosis. The unconscious mind is beyond our control and awareness. Let us continue to search for the truth about the mind, let us learn how to cope with our mental problems or how to avoid them, and we would live comparatively happier lives. Happiness is the goal in life and our mind must be free from unnecessary problems and unnecessary fears to find and enjoy happiness of the highest possible degree.

2 INFLUENCE ON MIND VERSUS HEREDITY

"Influence is to be measured not by the extent of surface it covers, but by its kind" - Channing

The mind is designed by nature to be different, to function at different levels. The mind is an abstract term and must not be confused with the word "brain". The mind is an abstract quantity like an idea whereas the brain is a tangible quantity. However, the mind, like ideas, can be measured qualitatively if not quantitatively.

The concept of mind is inconclusive. What is mind in its functional form? Mind is consciousness, individuality, personality, inner life, soul, whichever it is. It is the mind that gives a person his individuality or his personality, his character. Mind is probably best described as the life of a brain, for without brain there is no mind, hence no life of the body, as is in the case of a deceased person. The mind perceives, interprets data brought in by the sensory organs: the eyes, ears, nose, skin and tongue. It analyzes, judges, knows, creates, memorizes, visualizes, reasons, intuits and emotes. It is actually the person itself; it makes a person different from non-living things which have no brains, hence no mind.

Mind, like the person, grows as a person grows in height and weight, or size. The mind grows in its ability to perceive, to memorize, to make correct judgments, to visualize, and even to grow in sensuality. Minds, like people who are growing, grow to different levels and stop growing at different ages. Attempts to measure the mind through examinations, through I.Q. tests or performance or aptitude tests are popular and practical. Technically speaking, minds of gigantic size are minds of genius, dwarf-sized minds are either described as idiots, morons or imbeciles, depending on the level of smallness. The average mind is the commonest type and is to be denoted in psychological term as a mind with an I.Q. of 90 to 110.

Babies are equipped with an undeveloped mind, which develops in capability till it approaches adulthood. However, few babies can develop their minds to maturity fast enough to be able to look after themselves; babies, like morons or idiots, are completely innocent, and those who are matured at the age of two or three are prodigies or boy wonders - such prodigies are extremely rare. The mind grows from a completely useless, undeveloped form to maturity, whereby it could deal with the complexities of everyday life. How do minds grow? By trial and error, by practice. The mind is subject to all sorts of impressions and sensibilities; it favors some of these and abhors the others, or it could take them for granted. But we know that impressions do leave a mark on our minds, as is evident in human behavior. Why are we sometimes prejudiced, sometimes well-disposed? The answer is that impressions leave different marks on our mind - some affect our ego for the worse, some for the better. It is natural to favor those which satisfy our ego-needs; those which destroy or hurt our ego, we describe as harmful or evil influences and we hope to be rid of such evil influences.

How do we account for personalities or personal characteristics? Look at the born genius. Look at the lazy good-for-nothing. Look at the honest, the grateful and the good. Scrutinize the criminal, the thief, the murderer and the idiot. Are they not as different as white is from black? They are indeed! And you can find them from all social classes, from all over the world, from all communities. You may say that certain inborn factors, genes and the nervous system account for the different levels of mentalities, of personal integrity, of uprighteousness. If you say that clever parents breed clever children, you can be proved right, but you can still be proved wrong, for feeble-minded children do exist in families where the parents or even the grandparents and great grandparents are or were bright. It may seem that inborn factors contribute to personal characteristics such as cleverness, feeble-mindedness, honesty and criminal behavior. It may also be that environmental push or encouragement are responsible for individual development. A man's mind reflects his background.

True enough a "poor" environment produces a pessimistic, unhappy, discontented, problem-riddled person, whose behavior is probably hesitant, unsure or lacking in zeal. A favorable environment, an environment where culture exists, results in self-confident, alert, clever people; but there are exceptions and we find criminally inclined, feeble-minded individuals in a comparatively well-off society. It may be that inborn factors are lacking in such individuals whose environment is favorable to healthy, normal development. Generally, clever parents do have clever children, and most clever children come from the upper classes of society, as studies by Lewis Terman and Hollingworth show. It is up to the reader to observe in his life the above- mentioned and confirm what has been said. Statistics can be deceiving.

3 THE EMOTIONS

"Man is the only animal that laughs and weeps; for he is the only animal that is struck with the difference between what things are, and what they ought to be" - William Hazlitt

Basically, there are five emotions: happiness, sorrow, love, hatred and anger. Technically speaking, we experience certain emotions when electrical impulses affect certain parts of our brains. The brain can be divided into centers, e.g., the pleasure center, the happiness center, the sorrow center and the anger center.

At any time, if we are conscious, we are harboring at least one emotion; we are happy at times, sad for want of companionship at other times, passionate sometimes and feel hateful and angry when offended or when offensive thoughts intrude our consciousness. However, we are capable of feeling more than one emotion. We can feel angry and yet love at the same time, sad and yet happy; these are mixed emotions. The seat of emotions is the conscious mind. Certain people tend to feel more of one emotion than another. That is why some people are often cheerful and happy, while some are chronically melancholic.

Emotions are either good or bad. The good emotions are happiness and love and they are good in that they make others happy as well. The undesirable emotions of hatred, anger and sorrow all contribute to make an individual a swearing, cursing, frustrated, hesitant, reluctant person who finds that the undesirable emotions are presenting undue obstacles to his progress while robbing him of his stability, concentration and peace of mind. These undesirable emotions can be so great and unbearable that in extreme cases the individual would end his own life in an attempt to eradicate them. Whereas happiness contributes to health and normal development, undesirable emotions can lead to sickness and even diseases as they may rob the individual of his appetite and his desire to look after himself. In short, they may induce personal denial or neglect. That is why melancholic people are seldom fat - they are thin and may even present an emaciated appearance.

4 CONCEPT FORMATION

"Order and reason, beauty and benevolence, are characteristics and conceptions which we find solely associated with the mind of man" - Karl Pearson

Concepts are ideas held by the mind to be true and the formation of such concepts starts from childhood and continues till a person dies. We are exposed to so much influence that we have many ideas about many different things, such as happiness, or love, for example. Concepts provide notions and views about things in life; concepts color our lives and make us what we are. Concepts help us in our search for the meaning in life. They help us in our work towards certain goals, they help make us our charitable selves, our cooperative and helpful selves, or they help make us filial sons or daughters or Machiavellian individuals. Evidently, different people hold different concepts and also different quantities of concepts.

It is the conscious mind which forms all the concepts and an intellectual would obviously hold more concepts and form more concepts than a non-intellectual, for an intellectual's mind is the mind which finds great satisfaction or pleasure in the formation of concepts. Intellectuals have so many concepts about so many things that the average person tends to admire him.

5 THE AESTHETIC SENSE OF THE MIND

"A thing of beauty is a joy forever; its loveliness increases, it will never pass into nothingness" - Keats

The mind classifies things as either beautiful or ugly, or "in-between". We can discern beauty in nature, in animals, and even in ideas. Beauty is, however, relative; e.g., if everybody had the same features or the same mentality, would there then be beauty? Certainly not. Because things vary in appearance, size and what-not, they affect us differently; some make us feel uneasy, such as dark objects, since darkness may be associated with evil; some things please us with their appearance.

Animals are considered inferior to human beings, in intellect as well as in form or appearance. Who would compare himself to an animal? Would it not be self-debasing to do so? How do we know that animals do not consider human beings ugly creatures? Our ideals or prototypes of beauty influence our judgment of beauty. To one person, a picture or a portrait may be beautiful, to another it may not be considered so. We all have the prototype of beauty in our mind; we may have in mind the beauty of an actress whom we admire, and whose beauty we expect others to approve, or we may consider someone beautiful as long as her vital statistics approach that of Miss World, and the features of whose face are as regular and outstanding as the beauty queen's. Even in designing the model of a car, we have a prototype of the perfect model in mind, and, of course, we may make alterations here and there, believing that we can make the model more perfect.

We even have prototypes of ugly characters or personalities. We have ideals of the perfect heights for both men and women, and even ideal weights. We have in short a prototype of the perfect life in our mind, and we steer the path of life as far as possible along the lines of this perfect life. Human beings tend to have prototypes that are too far advanced and complex to be realized and in real life are always short of the perfect satisfaction.

6 THE INTELLECTUAL

"Mind is stronger than matter, mind is the creator and shaper of matter; not brute force, but only persuasion and faith is the king of this world" - Carlyle

One person is always expressing his ideas and often analyzes things; another could not make heads or tail out of ideas or situations and has nothing interesting to say. The first person has an innate or acquired desire to perceive through the faculty of reasoning; his intellectuality is either natural to him or the result of intellectual training such as university education or higher education.

Reason undoubtedly must be detached from prejudice in to be worth the energy of the mind; reason of a prejudiced character may be worthwhile only to the individual who conceives it and repugnant to the one whom it "touches". The "repelled" individual would hence have a reason to do to the conceiver of the prejudice what he deserves, be it slander or personal attack, or a strong attack upon his ideas, thereby resulting in undesirable conflict. The intellectual must always act with unprejudiced reasons or notions in order to win the respect of his fellow-men.

The intellectual is a keen observer of the intricacies of situations and knows what they are all about. He thus knows how to act accordingly. His interest is uncommon; he favors reasoning and does not give in to his emotions. He likes to reason things out for himself and as subjects like politics, religion or science need reasoning to grasp, he enjoys these subjects. A man of intellect often cannot be persuaded without the use of reasoning; he does not take things for granted. He wants to find out for himself; he thus reads and asks lots of questions to get satisfactory answers. His abundance of mental energy, his zeal for knowledge, all make him expressive as well as impressive.

The intellectual genius awes people with his superb mental power, his ideas and his imagination; he is essentially capable of complex thinking involving the most abstract of concepts and he is a keen observer of relationships between ideas and concepts and between objects. He is different from the rest in that his power of abstraction and creation is much greater. Intellectual giants command the respect of other people but at the same time they may appear as stupid to some who are incapable of grasping their far too advanced ideas and may be branded as heretics.

7 THE PREJUDICED MIND

"It would be well for all of us to remember that suspicion is far more apt to be wrong than right and unfair and unjust than fair. It is a first cousin to prejudice and persecution and an unhealthy weed that grows with them." - Dr. Francis J. Braceland

The prejudiced person would never make a good, reliable thinker. Narrow minded and guided more by emotion than by reason, he is certainly irritating. The prejudiced person is essentially an egoistical person who is selfish and is not willing to let others control him easily. Bear in mind that not all egoistical people are selfish; some are helpful, cooperative and willing to do justice to people. Why are prejudiced people irritating? Because they are egoistic. A person would find a biased person irritating because their egos clash, because the essentially egoistical person finds that the prejudiced person does things that affect his self-respect or self-worth. The prejudiced person out of selfish ego needs, does things that are inconsiderate towards another's ego or feeling, thus provoking a feeling of injustice or being let down or victimized. Prejudiced people in solving problems tend to find the easier, shorter way, so that their egos do not have to suffer the drudgery of labor.

Prejudiced people do things to appease or please their egos. There is always the consistent fear of the ego being troubled by even the slightest provocation or the slightest imminence of unpleasant element. The ego incorporated in the mind, automatically imposes a barrier to bar the ego from the abhorring influence. However, the prejudiced person is too in love with himself to be aware of this fact. That is why his ideas tend to be narrow, superficial and based only on those facts that are acceptable to his ego. He is afraid of hurting his ego in the drudgery of seeking the actual facts. He has a sincere desire to please his ego through being accepted by other people and through a fine self-image, hence his desire to please others, while still maintaining rigidly his self-respect, through adopting their prejudices and conceptions; he tries not to be eccentric and to be as acceptable as possible. There is therefore the tendency for prejudice to coincide with the lack of originality or novelty and lack of variety of ideas. Moreover, prejudice may be related to a low mentality.

8 INTROVERSION AND EXTROVERSION

"In each of us there is a little of all of us" - Lichtenburg

Introversion is an ingoing attitude of the mind, the direction of the energies of the mind inwardly. The introvert thinks but does not act. The introversion of a person is due to nature. The introvert can accept himself as his best friend and does not rigorously seek the friendship of others. The thinking man, the brooding man, the man who lives in a world of his own, of ideas mixed with feeling and emotion, the introvert is serene and gives the impression of being moody or glum. The introvert appears as a person with a withdrawn personality. He creates the life he wants for himself through the imagination and power of his mind.

The extrovert, who is a person with an outgoing personality, lives yet another sort of life; unlike the introvert, he lives the life that society creates. He seeks friends, he needs their opinions, he needs to see them and he needs to make them feel happy, for only then can he be happy. He longs for parties, social outings and picnics. He sees and lets what he sees provoke or rouse him instead of giving in to ideas or his imagination. He tends, in short, to love people, the world, society itself. He has a strong herd-instinct. He is what he sees in others.

But introversion and extroversion are not the only aspects in which personality can be analyzed. People are either introverts or extroverts, or they are in between, ambiverts, as they are called. Mostly, ambiverts prevail over the rest. The need to be alone sometimes and the need to seek friendship and companionship take their turn to affect the lives of mortals. We do not create an ideology for what sort of human being we should be, but whatever we are, be it introverts, ambiverts or extroverts, it is unimportant as long as we can still maintain the standard of happiness that is desirable to lead a satisfied life.

However, it seems that great thinkers are mostly introverts, for great thinkers must be willing to forego all other means of enjoyment for the enjoyment of creating ideas out of their imagination and creative power. But not all introverts are great thinkers. Many introverts are, unfortunately, prejudiced, spoiled by their own feelings or emotions, which overwhelm all the other faculties, especially the faculty of reasoning. On the other hand, extroverts with their experience of the outside world can deal with situations involving people better and may even be more imaginative and creative than introverts.

Therefore, whichever category of "vert" you may be, live with it and do not let emotion or feeling rule over you ultimately.

9 THE INSANE MIND

"Every man carries within him a potential madman" -
Carlyle

To understand the insane really well, one should have the
chance to be insane once, for only then would one know how
it is like to be insane. But then, it may not be possible, as an
insane person might not be aware of his own existence. The
insane person might feel that he is somebody great. He might
feel that he is on top of the world. The insane person might
feel either deep emotion or no emotion at all. He might be
very egoistical or have no ego at all. In any case, his mind
deviates too much from the normal and has lost its power of
control and reasoning. It is a mind running wild, knowing no
destination, even causing self-destruction.

Insanity has levels. The slightly insane may be obsessive or
compulsive; such a person may feel a compulsion to do
something even if it is against reason, or he may be troubled
by certain obsessive feelings or thoughts. Going higher up,
we have the schizophrenic type of insanity; the split
personality of the schizophrenic may cause drastic mood
swings in the individual, making him extremely happy and
talkative one moment and extremely sad, quiet and gloomy
the next moment.

Finally, we have total insanity: total insensibility to reason
and truth. This is the extreme stage of insanity and the insane
person provokes much more pity than hatred in other people.

Insanity then, is unnatural. It is also rare. It is the result of
the unconscious mind at work and factors such as extreme
stress and deep personal problems are responsible for the

breakdown of the mind. Insane people must be given special treatment and must be isolated from the rest in order not to frighten or cause harm to other people and for their own safety. It is sadistic to laugh at insane people mumbling to themselves. Furthermore insanity can also be hereditary due to genetic defects.

10 THE DEPRESSED, THE MELANCHOLIC AND THE MOODY

"The mind has great influence over the body, and maladies often have their origin there" - Moliere

Life is beset with problems. Some people treat their problems lightly. Others take them too seriously. When a person treats his problems too seriously, he becomes depressed or moody. Sometimes, a setback is so great that a person becomes greatly troubled with sorrow and is said to be depressed. The death of a loved one, the failure to gain love or recognition which the individual needs so badly, the failure to gain success, et al., all contribute to bring about a manic depressive state.

There are people who are born with a constitution that is melancholic. These people do not feel at ease with themselves. They feel discontented and unhappy with life. They feel gloomy and dull and their gloominess is chronic. Such people are melancholic people. They are unduly pessimistic and seldom optimistic. They are by nature quiet, serene and hard to arouse. They like to keep aloof and observe. Being of a contemplative nature, they naturally tend to be philosophical and idealistic about life. They are hard to satisfy as they are idealistic. They choose friends who are their kind and prefer to be in their company. They need a lot of sympathy and would exchange sympathies with friends who are similar to them.

The melancholic is by nature moody and depressed. However, people who have received setbacks and who are feeling rejected and sad are not to be taken for granted. They are the depressed people who need help and it is our duty to see that they receive due help and sympathy as friends.

11 THE HONEST MAN

"No legacy is so rich as honesty" - Shakespeare

The honest man does not yield to temptations to gain personal property or wealth through the easiest and the shortest but wrong way. The honest man believes in hard work and works hard if he sincerely wants to gain success or happiness. He abhors lying, cheating or stealing. He favors honest people and is happy that he is honest. He feels an inexplicably deep satisfaction if he returns to someone an item, e.g., his wallet or his watch, which has been left behind. In short, it can be said that he feels one of the greatest pleasures when he carries out an honest deed.

The honest person may however feel a temptation to keep what belongs to others, but his will power and his reason are strong enough to prevent him from yielding to the temptation.

Self-pride may prevent the person from yielding to such temptations. His sincere desire to keep a good impression, his desire to maintain his dignity, goes to make him an honest individual.

Also, the fear of being reproached, or, fear of the law, makes him adopt an "honest" attitude.

He may also feel that he should not steal or keep other people's property if he does not want other people to steal or take away his property.

Furthermore, his conscience, his moral sense, may prompt him to be honest.

Upbringing produces honest people too. If taught to be honest by parents or teachers while a child, a person may grow up to be honest and behave honestly; honest behavior can become habitual, like the bad habits of smoking and gambling.

12 THE CRIMINAL AND THE DISHONEST

"You must not lose faith in humanity. Humanity is an ocean. If a few drops of the ocean are dirty, the ocean does not become dirty." - Mohandas K. Gandhi

It is believed that criminal behavior can be the result of wrong upbringing. How can children brought up by parents to steal and lie and who have seen their parents committing such offences not imitate them? When such behavior becomes habitual, the criminal mind deceptively justifies its sinful acts and a hardened criminal might feel at ease with his conscience and carry on stealing or robbing without much thought of wanting to stop altogether and turn over a new leaf. The criminal behavior, once it becomes habitual, is hard to stop.

The environment and circumstances such as poverty makes an individual want to rob and steal. This seems to the materially deprived the easiest and surest way of solving their problems. But they may not realize that they might be robbing someone who is just as needy as they are. After all many who are rich have worked hard, at the expense of health and fun, and if their wealth is removed by robbers, they may suffer intolerable great anguish of mind. But the criminal is usually too selfish to realize this.

Do these criminals think that after using criminal means to gain they could maintain their happiness? No doubt, they might be happy with their newly and dishonestly acquired wealth, but how long would their happiness last? Before long, the law would probably start hunting them down and they would find themselves living in constant fear.

13 THE NEUROTIC

"The mistake which is commonly made about neurotics is to suppose that they are interesting. It is not interesting to be always unhappy, engrossed with oneself, ungrateful and malignant, and never quite in touch with reality." - Cyril Connolly

A person who counts his money over and over again, checks the tap repeatedly, looks at his watch and repeatedly observes the time is said to be neurotic. He is overcautious, obsessive and anxious.

The neurotic uses up vast amounts of nervous energy. The neurotic can either find it hard to gain success or his neuroticism can make him a conscientious, hardworking, ambitious individual who easily climbs his way to success. When the mind of the neurotic gives him unnecessary trouble with obsessions, the neurotic feels that he is losing control of his mind and is on his way to a total loss of control, and this would inevitably cause anxiety or even anguish of the mind. When the nervous system is upset in this way by obsessions or compulsion, the person is described as neurasthenic, sick in the nerves; the neurasthenic is very susceptible to a nervous breakdown.

On the other hand, if the individual's abundance of nervous energy is well attuned towards work of importance such as studies or steps to gain higher success, e.g., in the sphere of politics or science, then neuroticism would be an advantage rather than a disadvantage. In history, Hitler and Bonaparte had proven to be successful neurotics who had worked their way up. If the neurotic is constantly and "reasonably" pre-occupied or obsessed with the desire to achieve great success or the means of achieving outstanding success, then he is fortunate to be born neurotic; otherwise he would merely be an eccentric individual with undesirable habits.

14 THE SUPERSTITIOUS

"In all superstitions, wise men follow fools" - Francis Bacon

Why do people fear the number "thirteen" or regard black cats as the embodiment of the devil, believing that they would bring bad luck?

Superstitions have their influence on people's minds since childhood when the mind is most susceptible to influence. In our youth, our elders tell us stories of bad luck such as the "black cat"
myth or the "unlucky number thirteen" myth so that we grow up with these myths embedded in our mind, accepting unreasonable, baseless beliefs about certain omens or objects and their influence in the lives of men. However, with maturity, superstitions may wear off.

Conservative, illiterate people tend to be superstitious, being narrow in urbane experience and outlook; they tend to take things for granted. An educated person, who has learnt to think for himself, however, questions the superstitions and the rationale behind these beliefs. Superstitions have their origins in the past and are necessarily related to witch-craft or sorcery. In the Middle Ages, witches were known to work spells with certain objects and bad luck was associated with certain omens or occurrences such as hooting owls and preying vultures. Witches were then common in England and were feared and held responsible for many eerie and frightening events, so much so that a law evolved to burn witches at the stake. As a result, till this day, certain rituals and traditional taboos still affect our lives, making us slaves of passed-down superstitions, which are often associated with bad luck.

15 COMPLEXES

"A body seriously out of equilibrium, either with itself or with its environment, perishes outright. Not so a mind. Madness and suffering can get themselves no limit." - George Santayana

The inferiority complex is perhaps the commonest of all the complexes. All of us have some feelings of inferiority. Some of us feel insecure because of a low social or professional status. Some of us are short or thin and feel inferior because of this. When we are obsessed with a problem, such as lack of height or success, we are said to be suffering from an inferiority complex.

The problem of inferiority complex has a deep-rooted origin and manifests itself from childhood. A child is most receptive to adult influence and is easily taken in by their comments. A careless teacher's remarks about a child that he is stupid may cause more harm than it may seem. Many adults who presume that young children do not take things too seriously are quite careless at times in passing comments. But an intelligent, sensitive child is set thinking by others' comments and may begin to feel an inferiority complex, a sense of worthlessness. The destructive comments may leave their mark in the child's mind and are responsible probably for the workings in the unconscious mind that keeps troubling the poor child in some form such as dreams of success or achievement. We know that the unconscious mind affects the conscious mind and in this case it would induce in the conscious a feeling of inferiority.

The child might have had an unhappy childhood and might have been unpopular, e.g., he was not accepted as a play-mate by most of the other children and had kept aloof. The uncomplimentary remarks of the other children, coupled with those of the teachers or the parents who did not show much parental love and care, would make the pitiful child feel unwanted. He would wonder about the cause of his unhappiness and would probably attribute his lack of social success to an undesirable personality, an inferior personality, inferior in intellectual and character qualities, or even in appearance or size. This inferiority complex is bound to remain with him until adulthood or until success or social recognition is gained.

People with an inferiority complex tend to be ambitious; they would like to prove their worth, their "superiority"; such people feel uneasy in the company of others and might even become anti-social. People like Hitler or Bonaparte, had through marked feelings of inferiority, driven themselves to power and status. In fact, Napoleon Bonaparte became emperor of France. Although an inferiority complex makes one feel uneasy and unhappy for unjustifiable reasons, it has the advantage in that it motivates one to achieve considerable success. There is always a danger, however, that a person suffering from an inferiority complex would have gone to the other extreme of enjoying a superiority complex when he who gains considerable success.

A superiority complex is just the opposite of an inferiority complex; it is pride and obsession with one's proven qualities which others do not or will not fail to admire. It is in short a complacent, self-satisfied feeling. There is no feeling of urgency in the superiority complex and it can easily lead a person to his downfall.

The last sort of complex is the "Oedipus" complex. A boy may harbor a special feeling towards his mother and become jealous that his father is getting his mother's affections and he has a fear that his father may castrate him. This fear might cause him persistent uneasiness, and he would be said to be suffering from an "Oedipus" complex.

16 THE HYPOCHONDRIAC

"Mentally and bodily endowed men are the most modest while, on the other hand, all who have some peculiar mental defect think a great deal more of themselves" - Goethe

Everyone should be concerned about his health and maintain the highest possible standard of hygiene and try to keep fit. A person can keep fit by having a suitable diet, a good, clean environment and regular exercise. He can be a fitness buff: he can lift weights regularly or he can jog several kilometers a day; he can have regular medical check-ups; he can avoid drugs, cigarettes, liquor and the like; he can ensure that he has sufficient rest. Doing all these is alright if it were only a pre-occupation and not an obsession.

On the other hand, there are some people who are unduly and overly concerned about their health. They fret over the smallest things concerning their health. They imagine that they are suffering from some sickness or disease. But they may be in perfect physical health. They are simply obsessed with the state of their health. We call such people hypochondriacs. The hypochondriac does not behave rationally, as his so-called "sickness" or "disease" is only imaginary.

There have been cases of hypochondriacs who imagined or felt so strongly about their "sickness" though they were in perfect physical health that they subsequently developed symptoms of their imagined "sickness". We call such sickness "psychosomatic", which means that they are caused by the mind, and not by any viral infection or bodily infirmity. In fact, their sickness or disease can be cured, not by a medical doctor but by a psychiatrist.

The hypochondriac is actually a neurotic person.

17 INTELLIGENCE AND THE GENIUS

"Doing easily what others find difficult is talent; doing what is impossible for talent, genius" - A. Miel

Man is born with a certain degree of mental capacity. One may have the mental capacity of an idiot or a moron, the brain-power of a genius or just normal intelligence. It is believed that genes are responsible for the makeup of our mentality. Born with idiotic or moronic genes in the right combination, one would be an idiot or a moron. If blessed with enough of genius genes in the correct combination, one would be a genius. Behaviors are classified as intelligent according to whether they bring the desirable and beneficial results to the individual concerned or to society. Intelligent behavior is but the result of good foresight, insight and discretion. The genius is equipped with "tons and tons" of intelligence. These blessings might not be made use of and a person equipped with these might only be regarded as rather average because society judges an individual through his achievements and through his contributions to the world. Certainly a man with contributions equivalent to those of Einstein, Newton or even Rembrandt is not to be regarded as average. Thomas Alva Edison said: Genius is one percent inspiration and ninety-nine percent perspiration.

Many of us ordinary mortals could have been geniuses had we the drive in us to achieve something great. Genius has often been regarded as the infinite capacity for taking pains or the capacity to concentrate all one's effort on a certain problem or set of problems at hand. Many geniuses had suffered from defects, either of the personality or the physique. Byron suffered from clubfoot which brought about his inferiority complex, John Keats suffered from consumption, Abraham Lincoln and Shelley suffered from depression and Napoleon lacked stature and suffered from a genital defect; they nonetheless spurred themselves to fantastic heights of achievement to compensate for the imperfections they experienced in life.

Genius is a term difficult to define. Can its meaning be restricted to just being extremely good in general ability or to being extremely capable of achieving success in a certain field, e.g., politics, science or mathematics? To restrict its meaning to either is wrong for it has been used to describe people of both types of ability. The term "genius" has been used to describe a person with a high intelligence quotient, which is derived from intelligence tests such as the Stanford-Binet tests and the Simon-Binet tests. It has also been used to describe a person who achieved outstanding success in some field with the use of the intellect, e.g., men like Abraham Lincoln and Winston Churchill have been described as political geniuses.

Geniuses have long been regarded as people who are queer, sickly, or abnormal. But research by Lewis L. Terman, a famous American psychologist, has disproved this. Terman found bright children to be attractive, normal, superior in health, adaptable and socially normal. The notion of geniuses as being high-strung, nervous, sickly and unhappy is a narrow one, based on casual observation. True, many great men were abnormal, but not all. Some may seem abnormal because we do not understand or agree with them. But once we understand them and get along well with them they do not appear abnormal anymore. Such people might be the result of over-protectiveness, unsuitable home environment or even the desire to be abnormal.

Genius is rare. Its possession is happiness - that is what people normally think. This need not be true. A person endowed with an unusual degree of intellectual power is happy only when the other aspects of his personality are normal. If he is too sensitive, too nervous or unsociable, he is unhappy because his fellow-men fail to respect him as a normal human being though they might respect him for his marked intellect. A person of genius lives at a higher level of life. His interests are different, his modes of thought and argument differ from the common stock and as such, he is less likely to be understood than the common man. His arguments or thoughts may not make sense to most of us on account of its great intellectual depth. The mechanical efficiency of his brain is probably extremely great. Impulses that travel to the brain are probably plentiful and the brain is probably highly receptive of these. Genius could be attributed to a fine, efficient nervous system.

Men have become geniuses through feelings of inadequacy, e.g., men such as Napoleon Bonaparte and Lord Byron. A person may utilize his talents to compensate for some inadequacy to such an extent that genius results. Genius is also the ability to concentrate completely on the task at hand, thereby achieving great ultimate success.

Genius is the high intellectual ability to achieve great success in any field and it is a desirable and admirable quality.

18 THE PSYCHOLOGY OF LOVE AND HATRED

"Mind is the partial side of men; the heart is everything" -
Rivarol

Love creates love. Hatred provokes hatred. There are many types and qualities of love; we have paternal love, maternal love, fraternal love and sexual love. We love a person for some reason or other. We can love a person out of pity or even out of the feeling of necessity. For example, one may be a bad son or an unfilial daughter, but that does not mean one's parents will love one less; they may be angry but they do not hold any grudges or hatred, but may naturally feel responsible and concerned; this is a love or attachment which may be hard to explain. Such love is paternal love if it is from the father and maternal love if it is from the mother, and may generally be called parental love. Less in intensity is fraternal love: brotherly or sisterly love. The feeling of one brother towards another is a love attachment, less intense in nature, than parental love. It binds brothers and sisters within a sphere of unity, the family unit.

One can also love a friend as one loves one's brother or one's sister. This love is less permanent, less intense than fraternal love, but is important for it gives one meaning in life, e.g., the desire to help a friend whom one loves very much may give one much meaning in life.

Next we have sexual love, an intense kind of love that binds one to a member of the opposite sex; here the libido is at play. This love results in marriages, makes life-partners out of women and men. It makes a woman and a man share all the blessings and misgivings of life together, to tolerate and to be devoted to one another.

One can hate a person out of love or out of something repugnant that he has done. If, e.g., one found one's spouse unfaithful, one would feel some antipathy towards him or her, a mild feeling of hatred, but at the same time one still worries about him or her because of love. Alternatively, a person whom one does not love might have done something very offensive wherein one has the desire to beat him up, or, wishes him ill, harboring hatred towards him. This is deep, intense hatred which is anger with ill-disposed desire or wish directed towards the object of one's hatred.

Feelings of hatred need not be directed at people only; they can be directed at inanimate objects or occasions as well.

19 FEAR

"The mind is its own place, and in itself can make a heaven of hell, a hell of heaven" - Milton

People fear because they fear the undesirable consequences that can be brought about by the objects of their fear. In short, people fear because they fear harm to themselves or their lives; they fear pain, so they fear torture or punishment.

What is fear? Fear is the anxiety that results from anticipation or awareness of imminent or possible harm or pain. Fear prevents a person from functioning normally; it upsets his appetite, upsets his peace of mind and hastens his pulse rate. Fear is as undesirable as death, pain or suffering and fear is suffering itself. That people are afraid of fear is true, that people try to avoid fear is also true. Fear is very common and the person who knows no fear is a fool. On the other hand, a person who fears is the person who knows the dangers and knows how to avoid the dangers and also does things that involve the least of dangers.

Can fear be overcome? Certain people are naturally afraid of heights or dark places; certain people are afraid of strangers; such fears are hard to explain but are natural and may have their origins in the unconscious mind. Certain fears can be overcome, e.g., fear of failure or fear of falling from a great height. It is true that constant success in examinations eliminates the fear of failure. Practice on tight-ropes eliminates the fear of losing one's balance and falling off.

Fear can sometimes be so strong that a person is said to be suffering from a neurosis or nervous disorder. Fear has its origin in the unconscious mind and when it overpowers a person a nervous breakdown occurs; the person feels disturbed and restless, suffers from emotional conflicts and loses clarity of thought. Psychiatric help can unravel the cause of the problem that is troubling the patient's unconscious mind. The patient may be given occupational therapy so that he can "forget" his fears.

20 AMBITION

"Men are not prisoners of fate, but only prisoners of their own minds" - Franklin D. Roosevelt

As mentioned before, the mind is sensitive to impressions, likes and dislikes, love and hatred. It is our ambitions, coupled with ideals to be a perfect human being or to lead a perfect life, that inspire us to work hard and attain the goals set.

Parents could influence their children's future careers. Many children like to follow their father's "footsteps" which is natural. Ambitious parents do make their children feel that they have to be somebody, and encourage them to study and work hard. Children who are ambitious and want to be political leaders, doctors, lawyers or scientists are not to be taken for granted. But in the course of growth, certain changes are bound to occur such as changes in interests, careers or ambitions. Monetary gains may encourage a child or an adult to look for a lucrative career that may not be personally interesting to him.

Why are people ambitious? People are class conscious and classify professions as either professional, semi-professional, skilled, semi-skilled or unskilled. The professionals rank high in society. It is natural for people to aim for professional careers, such as engineering or law, so as to gain social esteem and to be able to live in material comfort and luxury.

Some people suffer from inferiority complex and feel themselves despised by others. They feel they have to prove their worth. They become ambitious and work hard to achieve their ends. In short everybody is ambitious, everybody wants to do something worthwhile in life, to do something he likes doing and which brings the utmost happiness.

21 INSPIRATION

"Man is equally incapable of seeing the nothingness from which he emerges and the infinity in which he is engulfed"
- Pascal

Inspiration has its highs and lows like the tide at the beach. At its highest level, inspiration overwhelms the mind, giving it a self-contained and self-satisfied frame which induces it to do that which it feels must be done. The inspired person performs a task with zeal and intense concentration.

However, at its ebb, inspiration produces little effect. The mind tends to be slack and unable to produce any creditable work.

Inspiration has made geniuses of men. Distinguished poets, famous novelists, great mathematicians, well-known scientists, renowned artists and talented musicians have been inspired to produce remarkable work. How does one account for the achievements of Mozart, Beethoven, Newton, Leibnitz, Gauss and Poincare, apart from ability?

Inspiration alone without effort produces nothing. Thomas Alva Edison, an inventive genius, has attributed his genius to "ninety-nine percent perspiration and one percent inspiration". Though hard work and ability are necessary for outstanding achievements, inspiration cannot be overlooked. Intense concentration can never be possible without inspiration, and it is only when the mind can concentrate that it can be efficient. Did not Byron or Shelley produce their wonderful poetic works out of inspiration which made them eager to express their feelings and emotions in lines and stanzas? Inspiration must be present in the genius in order to produce outstanding achievements.

There are things which bring about inspiration, love and admiration for example. Shelley wrote many of his poems out of love and his admiration of Lord Byron made him write a poem in praise of him. Natural and physical beauty have been known to inspire people to paint beautiful pictures in the field of art. Inspiration brings about an eager and strong desire to create certain things.

22 FEAR OF GETTING OLD

"Youth is a blunder, manhood a struggle, old age a regret"
- Benjamin Disraeli

When we are young, we want to be older. But when we are older, we are afraid of getting older. Why? When young, we tend to admire grown up people for their maturity and strength and wish to emulate them. As we get older and are approaching middle age, we know that we have stopped growing and are approaching the stage at which we may start "shrinking" and our intellect may lose its power; this "shrinking" is senile decay. Worse still, we are more aware of the imminence of death and increasingly wonder about the day we die and its consequences.

A person who reaches old age decreases in height at the rate of a quarter inch every four to eight years; he starts losing weight and his skin starts to roughen. His metabolism slows down and his blood vessels become less elastic, resulting in high blood pressure. His memory becomes weaker and the mechanical efficiency of his mind drops. He is prone to diseases and he finds it hard to recover from injury and disease. The aged person is frustrated as a result of being unable to do things that he did as a youth - his desires may be there, but his constitution may not permit him to satisfy his desires. Nonetheless, the old person acts wisely and is often calm.

Thus, old age is not desirable and people are afraid of getting old. People in old age tend to reminisce and regret that the younger days have passed so quickly.

23 PEOPLE AND FASHIONS

"Fashion is a form of ugliness so intolerable that we have to alter it every six months" - Oscar Wilde

There is a diversity of people living in this world today. People are diverse in origin, culture and language. More diverse still are their characters and mentalities. There will be more diversities in the future as people choose to be better than and different from each other. Personality and individuality, these are what people strive for.

The ways people dress often create impressions - fashion trends create impressions. The bell bottoms, the low-cut dresses and the mini/maxi skirts are not created for designing's sake; they are designed to please the eye. The designers may even design dresses that reveal certain parts of the body and thus bring out the attractiveness of the people who don the clothes. Certainly one expects the people of the twentieth century to dress differently from the people of the nineteenth or earlier centuries. But one does find some diehard conservatives who dress as nineteenth century cowboys or some late nineteenth or early twentieth century China-men. These are the outstanding people of society, outstanding not because of any achievement, but because they are great attention-getters. They are so proud of their conservatism, their old-fashionedness; they feel so different, so distinct from the rest of the world. They may be regarded by society as round pegs in square holes. But the fact that they stand out from the rest of the common people indicates their "uncommonness", their individuality.

In the sixties, males appeared more cissy, what with unisex dresses, flowery shirts and flashy pants. Ladies, on the other hand, appeared more manly. Alas, it did become more difficult to tell them apart from the men at times. But closer and keener observation proved that a "manly" female was indeed a female.

Shoes had then been getting higher at the heels, despite the fact that the people who wore such shoes were generally tall. Women had become taller, men were taller, boys and girls seemed taller. Was it because of too much hormones? No, the shoes had been taller. Thus, short men had become men of medium height, men of medium height had become tall and tall men had become practically giants.

In fact, our new fashion is the "old fashion", except for some modifications. It seems today to be fashionable requires us to look "old fashioned". This is no exaggeration or contradiction and is true. Sharp-pointed shoes give way to round-headed shoes which were a fashion in the past. Tight pants surrender to loose pants, short hair to long hair - the fashion of medieval times - and so on. In fact, new fashion gives way to old fashion. So, what is new fashion? Isn't it "old" fashion?

24 HYPNOSIS

"Life is the art of being well deceived" - Hazlitt

A person who has been hypnotized would respond according to the commands issued by the hypnotizer; he has temporarily lost his power of self-control - his conscious mind is asleep while his unconscious mind is at work. In fact, the state of hypnosis is comparable to sleep-walking. When a subject under hypnosis wakes up, he is not aware of what he has done under the influence of hypnosis.

A person who really does not wish to be hypnotized would never be hypnotized. The doctor or the expert in hypnosis would repeat certain commands over and over and the willing subject soon loses control of his conscious mind, leaving only the unconscious mind awake. The doctor could now pass commands to the unconscious mind and this would make the hypnotized subject do things that the doctor wants him to do. But he would not do the things he is afraid of doing, for the unconscious mind is the seat of fears.

Hypnosis is sometimes used on mental patients. People with deep seated problems such as great anxiety or sorrow are sometimes hypnotized into forgetting their problems. They would be told under hypnosis to reveal the causes of their problems; causes of mental problems such as anxiety and depression have their origins in the unconscious mind. The doctor could then find out the causes of the patient's problems and recommend remedial measures or treatments.

25 INTELLECT VERSUS EMOTION

"It is the mind that creates the world about us, and even though we stand side in the same meadow, my eyes will never see what is beheld by yours, my heart will never stir to the emotions with which yours is touched" - George Gissing

Our intellect reasons, analyzes, synthesizes and judges. Our emotion does none of these; it affects the intellect. When we are happy, we can reason out things relatively well. When we are sad or angry, we do not try to reason out things and we may even act unreasonably, e.g., when we are angry we tend to feel more irritated and tend to find faults with others more easily. This is against the dictates of reason.

Moreover, our intellect receives information from books or from our personal experiences and makes use of the information thus derived to create and to act accordingly. The emotion is affected by our experiences and also by the books we read and makes us feel at ease or uneasy. It does not create new ideas nor invent new things nor conform to our needs. When we need to be happy, it is not our emotion that makes it so, but our intellect that enables us to act according to our needs.

As is described above, our emotion is greater than our intellect in terms of influence. When we feel a certain emotion, we normally have a certain desire or set of desires and the intellect enables us to achieve the objects of these desires. In fact, emotion and desire are so closely related as to affect us almost instantaneously, that we tend to regard them as one emotion or feeling. When we are angry with somebody, e.g., we feel like scolding or beating up that person. But our intellect intervenes and makes us realize whether it is the right or reasonable thing to do. However, our emotion can be so strong that reason is out of the question; that is how people commit murder on the spur of the moment for which they live to regret or feel sorry later. When we are happy, we want to enjoy ourselves, e.g., in the cinema or at a friend's house. When we are sad, we want neither of these but to be alone, but our intellect would say that it is not good to be sad and we should enjoy ourselves, i.e., we should "forget" our sorrows and take a walk in the park or visit a good friend.

Therefore, it is true that the emotion rules our lives whereas the intellect enables us to realize the objects of our emotion or desire.

26 IDOLATRY AND BELIEF IN GOD

"God puts something good and lovable in every man, His hands create" - Mark Twain

People in ancient times, mystified by nature, have been known to worship trees and rocks. This was due to ignorance. But today science has explained many of the natural phenomena, from the origin of the rocks to the origin of the universe, and we no longer feel the awe or the fear of inanimate objects. That is why the worship of trees and rocks is now practically non-existent.

From the beauty of the universe, of nature, of the human body, many have come to the conclusion that there is and there must be a superior being above us all: God. Today, it is this God whom many of us worship. God's existence cannot be explained scientifically and this makes God all the more seemingly powerful and awe-inspiring. If we could scientifically explain God's existence, it is doubtful that we would still worship Him or feel awe for Him.

Many attempts have been made at interpreting God. But nobody seems to have any idea how God exists. People have ascribed to the revelations of certain holy persons such as Buddha or the Prophet Mohammed who preached good and who professed the goodness of God. Hence there are followers of religions such as Buddhism and Islam wherein people worship God in their own way. For example, Christianity preaches the goodness of the world and shows how Jesus, the Son of God, had been sent to earth to save Man's soul. It also shows in its own way how the universe was a creation of God.

Belief in God, like idol-worship or nature-worship is intuitive. When we can conceive that a certain fact is true, that logic is true, that our senses are true, that we are what we are is true, so can we conceive the existence of God as true.

In our woes, in our fears, in our troubles, we normally seek comfort and consolation from our friends, relatives who can render their help and others who are better off. It is a natural tendency to appeal for help from those who are more capable and better off than oneself. We may even look towards God for help and guidance, as we conceive God to be absolutely powerful. This is when God acts as an emotional support to people who have felt uncertain and worried and who need to feel secure and optimistic. It is true that many have thanked God, at least in their hearts, for their success or gifts.

27 THE PSYCHOLOGY OF LEADERSHIP

"The real leader has no need to lead - he is content to point the way" - Henry Miller

A leader should prove himself more capable and more confident than the rest and should be able to assert himself. He should be able to stand up for what he thinks is right, to work hard and to make people work for him.

On the other hand, followers should respect their leaders for their qualities. If not the leader would be a leader only in name. The followers should feel that they are inferior to the leader in some important respects, such as the ability to command men, decision-making ability and so on. The leader should not be afraid of his men and should act bravely and confidently. He should be above average in intelligence, but not too intelligent, for genius sometimes makes fools of leaders; the ideas of geniuses are sometimes incomprehensible to average mortals and these are rejected as ridiculous or foolish. The leader should act wisely and maturely as though honesty and integrity are his great virtues. The followers therefore should realize that the leader is their intellectual peer; now and then an intelligent follower may think he is smarter and may cause a rebellion or mutiny. On the other hand, if the leader proves himself to be too tyrannical and incapable rebellion or mutiny is inevitable.

Leaders should have personality and a sense of responsibility if they are to earn the respect of their followers. They should not attempt to do anything which they cannot do better than their followers. For example, an army officer who cannot outrun his men should not challenge them to a race. The leader should know how his men feel and act accordingly so as to keep up the morale of the men. He should accentuate his strong points and keep his weak points as far from sight as possible. Leaders should also be able to express their ideas freely and they should be able to speak well and clearly as well so as to create the impression of a capable leader.

Leadership ability can be acquired and comes with training. Those who like to be leaders will probably make good leaders and try to assert themselves over the rest. It is probably those who do not like to lead but who are forced to lead who make bad, inefficient leaders. However, a leader should not rule with the iron hand of fear as he would then be facing the danger of revolt or rebellion.

28 CONCENTRATION AND EFFORT

"Concentration is the secret if strength in politics, in war, in trade, in short, in all the management of human affairs"
- Emerson

All of us, at one time or other, must have found it utterly difficult to concentrate on the task at hand. The more effort we put in the more weary and dull we feel, our concentration is not any better and the mind feels sleepy and tends to be lazy, or it may wander off from the task at hand. This is inevitably due to the lack of interest.

On the other hand, an interested individual finds it easy and effortless to concentrate on the task at hand. If the interest is so great that as a result concentration is very much greater, then a person can be said to have reached the mental peak in his field of interest. Concentration is important in order to perform a task really well, and interest which is responsible for rapt concentration is thus important.

Concentration may be regarded as the power of attention. It is supposed that a person's power of concentration is never totally engaged; an average person may utilize only fifty to sixty percent of his power of concentration.

There are factors which prevent the individual from engaging his concentration as fully as he would like such as noises, emotional disturbances or the desire to other things. On the other hand, concentration may be so great as to render the person insensitive to outside noises. Emotional disturbances and the desire to do other things have a greater effect on concentration than outside disturbances. In such cases, the emotional disturbances and unwanted desires have to be eliminated before a person can concentrate on the task at hand. There are people whose concentration in certain tasks is so great that they attain the level of genius; examples are people such as Isaac Newton, Albert Einstein and Bertrand Russell. These people must undoubtedly have an overwhelming interest in the tasks at hand and the intellectual ability that is compatible with their interests.

29 THE EFFECT OF HARD WORK AND RELAXATION

"A sound mind is a sound body" - Juvenal

The mind needs rest; that is why we must sleep for a number of hours every day. We cannot expect the mind to work eighteen, twenty, twenty four hours every day. About one third of our lives is spent sleeping. Sleep is so essential that if we are deprived of it, we become irritable and disorientated and may even die.

An over-enthusiastic or over-ambitious person may work harder or put in more hours of work than is right for his nervous system. Such a person is bound to wear himself out too much and unless he gives himself sufficient rest, he is bound suffer in health, if not in mind. Due to prolonged fatigue, a person may develop tuberculosis or consumption or he may suffer from nervous disorders. When we are tired or fatigued we make more mistakes and feel more drowsy and less alert. We may even feel restless or uneasy - symptoms of nervous disorders - which may be followed by a nervous breakdown.

That is why we must pay as much attention as possible to relaxation as to work. Hard work is desirable for success, but it should be in reasonable quantity and should not deprive us of our health and well-being. Hard work should not be regarded as the only means to happiness, happiness being the ultimate aim in life, though it is a prerequisite for achieving success, while success may be regarded as the means of happiness.

30 THE EFFECT OF PAST EXPERIENCE ON THE MIND

"A man is sane morally at thirty, rich mentally at forty, wise spiritually at fifty - or never" - William Osler

The following is a common saying: Once bitten twice shy. It simply means that one would never try to repeat a mistake. From experience one knows one's strengths and weaknesses, what to expect and what not to expect of oneself and one's inclinations and tendencies. Therefore, one should avoid certain tasks or occasions for personal reasons, such as lack of capability, determination or confidence.

One's experience more or less makes one what one is, especially childhood experience. If one had a poverty-stricken childhood, one would probably grow up to be a thrifty adult. If one were born with a silver spoon in one's mouth, as an adult one would probably be generous or pleasure-loving. A person with strict parents would probably grow up to be a disciplined and self-reliant adult while the reverse would also be probably true. A person who had been a social outcast would probably grow up to be an anti-social adult.

A person's ability to respond or behave appropriately in a new environment is regarded as intelligence and this intelligence depends on past experience. As people's experiences differ, so too do their attitudes and their mentalities. For example, a person may have a conservative attitude because he has acquired it from his conservative parents. Without experience or lacking in it, a person is unsure of himself and is said to lack confidence or proficiency. Experience is important in that it enables one to act intelligently. An environment full of challenges and intellectual stimulation produces a bright individual while an uncongenial environment lacking in culture produces an individual who is short of brightness and alertness.

31 THE EFFECT OF EDUCATION ON THE MIND

"Mind unemployed is mind unenjoyed" - Bovee

In order to be efficient, a mind needs education, which could either be self or school education. People with intelligence would probably have "cultured" their outlook, learnt the common language, the histories and literatures, the sciences and mathematics. Intelligence is usually described as the ability to adapt to any situation. For example, the versatile Benjamin Franklin was self-taught as was President Abraham Lincoln.

Books and the printed idea influence our lives far more than we are aware of. Past experience in the form of books could also influence our lives. From books we build a world of fantasy. As we read novels and fairy-tales, encyclopedias and other factual books, we get our knowledge and wisdom. Without books, most of us would be dullards and would have little to say. Ideas in books stimulate our minds and make us think.

Books today are easier to print and are produced at a far greater rate and in greater quantities and varieties. Ideas are thus constantly passed on. In addition, we have libraries with a great variety of books and we have schools with better library facilities. In fact, today's world is a more cultured world. As books make us use our imagination or intellect, their importance should not be overlooked. History books or books of literature enable us to understand our predecessors and their times as well as to have a greater insight of life.

School education is important especially for young children

who need some guidance and "push". A teacher who instructs a student should be able to apply psychology to induce his student to study. He should act as a parent, a brother, a friend and a mentor to the student. A student might find books uninteresting or even boring. A teacher or lecturer should therefore make his lecture clearer, briefer and easier to understand; this would make it more interesting for the student. In addition, a student could easily satisfy his doubts or curiosity through his teacher who should be ever willing to help.

Too much emphasis on formality in education is not conducive to creativity, inventiveness or originality of thought. At its worst, it could be a hindrance to the far advanced student or highly gifted student. Gifted students learn the work far more quickly than the rest of the class. Thus gifted students may become bored and lose interest in their studies if they continue with the same system of education.

32 THE UNCONSCIOUS MIND

"Beauty in things exists in the mind which contemplates them" - David Hume

The word "unconscious" means "unaware". It seems that we have two minds, one is the conscious mind and the other is the unconscious mind. The unconscious mind seems to be more powerful than the conscious mind and exerts some form of control over the latter. The dreams we have are the results of the unconscious mind. At least, the conscious mind is within our control, and we are aware of its existence. The unconscious mind is beyond our control and is an entity by itself, and we are not aware of its functioning or existence.

Edmund Freud had carried out studies of the unconscious mind, so had Alfred Adler and other psychologists. The unconscious mind is the seat of our fears; it is that which is responsible for our feeling "troubled", restless or uneasy. Being beyond personal control, it is actually a "being" by itself, capable of causing trouble to the individual without his even knowing it, it is the "devil" within us. Analysis by an expert would enable us to bring it under control. Our dreams and our conscious thoughts are results of the unconscious mind, which exercises an invisible influence on the conscious mind. The unconscious mind produces ideas that are "realistic" but it lacks the power of reasoning or logic, unlike the conscious mind. It is responsible for the desires we harbor.

33 THE EGO

"Pride goeth before destruction and a haughty spirit before a fall" - Old Testament, Proverbs XVI-19

The ego is the awareness of self; it is reflected in the "I" attitude; it has its seat in the conscious mind. The ego does itself justice. If someone says you are a fool, you, your ego, says you are not one and tries to prove to him you are not. If someone deprives you of your happiness, your ego bids you to get it back. Your ego makes you what you are; it either make you a wise man or a fool, an honest citizen or a criminal. Without your ego you are not you, you are nothing or anything.

The ego makes you selfish; it makes you find happiness, wealth, luxury, love, pity, fun and so on. It makes you want to live, it makes you jealous and envious, it makes you angry, it makes you quarrel and fight. In short, it makes you look after and defend yourself.

Even in suicides, the ego plays a part. Because the ego could not stand the indignation of suffering and pain, the ego decides to put an end to it once and for all, and prompts its possessor to an attempt of suicide. In short, the ego abhors suffering and pain, but encourages fun and happiness.

Perhaps, nobody can be said to lack an ego, unless he is insane. Insane, really insane, people are incapable of looking after themself and thus can be said to have lost their ego.

34 THE MENTAL DEFECTIVE

"People have got so accustomed to having life seasoned with crime and poverty that they cannot contemplate a life without it" - George Bernard Shaw

Like the intellectual genius, the mental defective is extremely rare. Mental defectives lack the power of thinking and reasoning but they are not to be confused with the insane. They are capable of looking after themselves to some extent - at least they can satisfy the basic need for food and drink. But lacking the power of thinking and reasoning, they are incapable of anticipating danger or risk, and hence, fear; they only fear what they could anticipate, which are few.

Mental defectives are thought to be born so, but given special treatment and training, can be taught to do certain things, and hence improve quite considerably. There are different degrees of defectiveness. The worst and most defective are the idiots, followed by the morons and the imbeciles. Mental defectives are extremely slow in learning. Psychologists have discovered means of detecting mental defect; they devise I.Q. tests wherein an average child should be able to do certain things for his age; the child who is a mental defective is not capable of doing these things.

However, fortunately, mental defectives, like the genius, are extremely rare. They are a burden to the state as well as a social and family problem.

35 THE SNOB

"If there be a hell upon earth it is to be found melancholy in a man's heart" - Burton, Anatomy of Melancholy

The man who pulls up his nose at others whom he considers inferior is irritating to most of us. He is the snob, the man who has a high opinion of himself and is proud of himself, the man who is conscious of his "class", the man who never fails to try to impress people. If only he could impress people, if not irritate people.

There are many types of snobs. There are the intellectual snobs. There are the social snobs. There are the snobs who snub snobs. Snobbishness is a quality or rather an attitude of the mind. The intellectual snob is only a snob as long as he considers himself smarter than the rest, or if people consider him so. The social snob is only a snob as long as he has more property and more money than the rest. Devoid of the chance to prove themselves of their worth, snobs would not be snobs. It is true that certain people have a profound hatred for snobs and are either openly or secretly antipathic towards them; such people abhor the sight of snobs, and consider talking to snobs a waste of time, and hence, prefer to keep away from and feel proud in doing so. Such people, unknowingly, are also snobs; they are the snobs who snub snobs.

It appears that circumstances produce snobs. Not given the ingredients for its birth, snobbishness does not exist. Snobs do not want to be associated with those whom they consider inferior and they either mix with their equals or superior.

36 THE FANATIC

"Glad that I live am I; That the sky is blue; Glad for the country lanes; And the fall of dew" - Lizette W. Reese, A Little Song of Life

The fanatic is an overenthusiastic person. For example, the soccer fan who is crazy about soccer, the boy who is crazy about rugby, the man who is crazy about going to the pictures, et al.

Fanatical behavior is necessarily obsessive. There is the man who constantly talks about God or Religion. There is the man who is always talking about his car. There is the dictator who is always talking about being emperor of the whole world. These are fanatics, whose desires are constantly occupying their minds, or who find certain events or objects most interesting and feel compelled to talk about them.

The fanatic has little time for other things besides the objects which make them fanatical. Hitler was a political fanatic, so was Napoleon Bonaparte or Mussolini. Isaac Newton and Albert Einstein were scientific fanatics. In fact, geniuses are same sort of fanatics, men who are regularly occupied with certain tasks, men who could concentrate all their energies on these certain tasks. The fanatic has a definite aim in life, i.e., the aim to achieve success in that field which involves their most interesting subjects.

To us, the fanatics may seem crazy. But we know that at one time or another, most of us have been crazy about something, e.g., as boys most of us must have been crazy about toy-guns, or toy-trains. Fanatics would appear crazier if they try to achieve something which is quite beyond their capability.

37 THE HUMOROUS

"No man is really old until his mother stops worrying about him" - William Ryan

The humorous like to play and crack jokes and often laugh at themselves, at other people, or at their jokes. They are gay and hearty and superficial at times and they derive satisfaction from people who laugh with them.

The humorous person is essentially an easy-going, care-free person, an extrovert in nature. He is someone who loves people and enjoys the company of people. He is gifted with a well-developed herd-instinct. Seldom does he get angry or depressed.

Humorous individuals are apparently more common in the upper classes. Devoid of financial worries and material discomforts, they can adopt a self-satisfied, contented frame of mind, which enables them to treat life jokingly and lightly.

38 THE SHREWISH

"Hell knows no fury like a woman scorned" - Anonymous

The woman or man who loses his or her temper easily, who nags often or always finds faults with others, the shrewish seems fanatical about faults and mistakes. The shrewish shouts and screams, is violent at times, and disturbs the tranquility of the environment. A man possessed of a wife who is a shrew finds his life a hell and a woman with a husband like that would cry often.

The shrewish is an unhappy, moody, temperamental character, and if countered with equally shrewish manners may blow up in violence. To deal with a shrew, one needs to be patient, calm, sympathetic, and even apologetic at times, for shrewishness is the result of instability and disturbance of the mind.

39 THE JEALOUS AND THE ENVIOUS

"Man is so inconsistent a creature that it is impossible to reason from his belief to his conduct, or from one part of his belief to another" - Macaulay

Every one of us has been jealous or envious at one time or another. We would probably be jealous if a competitor or rival has the advantage over us. For example, the eldest child in the family may be jealous because his younger brother receives more attention from their parents, a lover would be jealous if somebody else is seen acting lovingly with his beloved. Now, envy is quite different from jealousy, in that it goes together with ill-will or malice; envy may be described as jealousy tinged with ill-will.

The cause of jealousy is over-possessiveness. The jealous person does not want rivalry, he wants security, he wants to feel that something or somebody belongs exclusively to him. He sees in rivals the insecurity of something he desires to be exclusively his. Jealousy is natural but it should not be so great as to induce the person to carry out foolish acts, such as doing harm to a rival; the person should rationalize with himself and fully realize that rivalry is inevitable in life.

40 REPENTANCE

"Superstition is the religion of feeble minds" - Burke

Sometimes, individuals feeling that they have done something their conscience would not justify, want to do something honest and philanthropic, or good, to compensate for the bad they had done. Such individuals, having realized their folly, their wrong, could not live happily with the thought of being wrong and sinful troubling their conscience. They want to eliminate this uneasiness of mind and they feel that by doing something opposite to sin they would feel more at ease. This is repenting, an act which criminals sometimes adopt.

The repentant person is the person who realizes that he is wrong and is willing to change his ways and in addition does something good and helpful in return for the trouble he has caused and the sins he has committed; he is the person who derives great satisfaction from resolving to be good to society.

41 BRAINWASHING AND INDOCTRINATION

"The mind is malleable. Brainwashing and indoctrination are hammering the mind into a certain shape." -
Anonymous

Man's mind is subject to impressions and even superstitions. Man, whether you want to believe it or not, is fickle-minded, but when we say that a person is fickle-minded, we speak in relative terms, meaning that he is more fickle-minded than the rest. Who is not a slave of the fashion of his age? Who is not influenced by books? Who has never changed his opinions? Who has never changed his hobbies or whose desires and likings have not changed with time? External things influence our likes more than we are aware of.

Books, speeches, orations, affect our intellects. Philosophers have been known to agree and later disagree with each other. Atheists have been converted to, e.g., Christians or Buddhists. People have been politically converted and have clandestinely given their support to certain political fighters. Had not the great Mao-Tse-Tung brainwashed many a non-communist so that they ended up as communists or behind bars because they displayed communist sympathies or distributed communist pamphlets. Hitler or Goebbels had been known to work up people to mass hysteria, in support of their intentions.

What is brainwashing? We have our prejudices. We have our needs and our instincts. Our instinct tells us we have to defend ourselves against our would-be aggressors, we have to be protected, we have to have economic and political security. Hitler, Geobbels, the genius of propaganda and Minister of Propaganda of the Third Reich, and, Soekarno, could work on the minds of the masses, making them feel the need of a strong government which has the support of the people, and hence gained the support of the people. In short, these dictators or leaders worked expertly on the instincts of the people, and this act of working on instincts is "brainwashing". Political leaders might use facts, figures and prophesies to provoke the masses to a higher level of national consciousness; Hitler's senseless slaughter of Jews in the Second World War was justified in his orations to the German Republic as an attempt to "purify" the Teutonic race, to preserve its superiority over other races, but psychologists had analyzed that Hitler actually had the Jews slaughtered to avenge himself of the injustice the Jews had done him when he was a youth. Hitler, reputedly a great orator, appealed greatly to the emotions of the Germans, working them up to high levels of hysteria and national pride. As a result, he was able to induce many a fit youngster to be drafted into the army and the youth corps. Mao-Tse-Tung came to power at a time when China was starving and disunited and when life was hard. Mao was able to appeal to the people and inspire new hopes in them; with his Marxist doctrines he promised the masses a productive, better life. He managed to win over the intellectuals and fought the Kuomintang hard to establish the Republic of China. Mao was also reputed as a great orator, a person who knew how to appeal to certain instincts of the masses.

Indoctrination follows the same principle as brainwashing. However, it is a longer process of brainwashing. Indoctrination is meant more for the intellectuals, the people who are harder to influence, the people who have their own doctrines. Indoctrination appeals to the intellect of the "victims" and establishes a radical influence upon the minds of the indoctrinated. Indoctrination could be carried out through carefully written books or pamphlets. The works of Karl Marx or Lenin when brought to the forefront of a China torn by civil wars had indoctrinated many intellectuals, who formed a movement to try to establish a government along Marxist or Socialist lines.

42 MIND OVER MATTER OR MATTER OVER MIND

"What is matter? Never mind." - Anonymous

The mind is so full of capabilities and potentialities, that it would not be a surprise if one day, men deify the mind, when the mind would be God.

The mind controls our body, the matter, but this is not absolute control. Can we, e.g., control our heart-beat or our breathing mechanism if we will it? We cannot. But it is the heart-beat and the breathing mechanism which keep us alive. Without the heart or the lungs, how do we live? It would be impossible to live, which means our mind would not live. Therefore, the heart and the lungs control the mind, i.e., matter over mind is true. Besides, without the brain, which is matter, there would not be mind.

But mind over matter is also true. Man could make use of inanimate objects or animals and his mind controls what he is doing, such as lifting his leg to kick a ball or lowering the arm to pick up a book from the table.

This question of whether mind is over matter had been a great philosophical problem which some philosophers had mulled over. The meaning of mind over matter is vague, hence making it easy to argue for or against it.

43 OPTIMISM AND PESSIMISM

"The optimist never says "die" while the pessimist says it often" - Anonymous

A successful business executive or a successful businessman has every reason to be optimistic about the future. With a high income and the success in his work, he has a better chance of achieving a host of other successes, such as, e.g., a happy home. How can we expect a beggar to be optimistic about the future? Certainly not. A successful man is confident and is thus optimistic; he knows he has the ability and his success proves it, and he knows that this ability can bring him more success in future.

On the other hand, a man plagued by failure, a man who did not do well in studies or work and who does not earn enough to support himself tends inevitably to be pessimistic. His lack of ability or lack of luck or opportunity is obvious to him and he dares not to expect too much, feeling as if he were born to live a life which is doomed to failure and unhappiness.

Probably, too frequent a blow would result in a pessimist as too often a success would evolve an optimist.

44 GREED

"To have enough is good luck, to have more than enough is harmful. This is true of all things, but especially of money."
- Chuang Tse

Greed may be manifested in such cases as stealing and robbery. Why would somebody who has a chance of earning a decent living want to rob a bank? Well, it can be greed, it can be the easy way out of financial worries, or it can be the easy way to earn a living. Why rob a bank? He could have robbed a shop or a store. Besides, the bank is guarded. The answer is probably greed. The bank is well-stocked with cash. Who does not want a vast supply of cash?

Everyone was born more or less greedy. We want more than enough of the necessities of life. This is because we want to feel secure. No amount of cash can be said to be enough; no millionaire or billionaire would say he has enough. Who is incapable of spending money and who has never exceeded his budget? A person might say that one million dollars would be enough to spend for a life-time, but given the opportunity, he would probably seek for more, for he knows that one million dollars can be as easily spent within a short time as one hundred dollars. The more wealth he acquires, the more secure and less worried he feels.

Greed is natural. But extreme greed is rare, just like lack of greed. The greedy man who spends little, who hoards, and who is very rich, is indeed queer; such a person may look upon the possession of wealth as the ultimatum of life and happiness itself, and probably finds little meaning in spending the wealth which he possesses.

---

45 SADISM AND MASOCHISM

"Sadists may be compared to animals, but this may not be a fair comparison, as animals do not enjoy seeing others suffer though they may enjoy them as food" - Anonymous

Sadism, the act of gaining satisfaction through seeing others suffer, is abnormal and is evidence of a sick mind. A sadist may be a person who has suffered considerably and who feels that the world has been especially unfair to him. He therefore derives satisfaction from seeing the world, his fellow-beings, suffer. Sadism may have other inexplicable origins or it can be inborn or natural just like criminal tendency.

Masochism, the behavior whereby the individual inflicts bodily pain to himself and derives pleasure from it, is also abnormal; it can also take the form of inflicting mental pain to the self through such measures as reading "sad" novels. There is no tendency for masochists to look for the normal means of pleasure, and masochists can be found practicing perverted acts such as homosexual acts.

46 HOMOSEXUALS AND TRANSVESTITES

"A man may dress and behave like a woman and vice versa, and we may thus fall in love with the wrong woman" -
Anonymous

Homosexuals are people who find sexual attraction in members of their own sex. If an individual is deprived of the normal means of sexual gratification for a prolonged period and only members of the same sex are available to him, he may gradually find an erotic attraction in the members of his own sex. In many cases, homosexuality is due to unforeseen circumstances; a jilted lover, e.g., may turn homosexual. The workings in the unconscious mind may also bring about a homosexual.

Transvestites are people who like to dress up or make-up like a member of the opposite sex, e.g., a man who dons skirts and blouses. The cause is probably the unconscious mind; it may be a manifestation of the desire to be a member of the opposite sex.

47 CONSCIENCE

"People who lack conscience may be compared to animals, but this comparison is wrong for animals do demonstrate conscience" - Anonymous

It is the conscience which makes us humane and distinguishes us more or less from animals. It is the moral sense, the sense of right and wrong, and it may also be regarded as the intuition, which enables us to sense other things such as truth, or the future, or what is to happen.

The conscience prevents us from robbing, stealing, killing or even lying. If the conscience is normal, then a person would act normally, but if he lacks the will-power to obey the biddings of his conscience, then he would be committing offences that might make him a hated person or a notorious or hunted criminal. There are many things we would like to do but which our conscience forbids us to do and sometimes against our conscience we do things which we later regret; this is because the temptation to do these things is too great. Fortunately, the conscience, much more often than not, holds an upper hand over us, otherwise the crime-rates would be extremely atrocious. The conscience works hand in hand with the intellect.

48 NARCISSISM

"John is always staring at the mirror. Is he admiring the image of himself? No, he is admiring the mirror!" - Anonymous

It is said that Narcissus saw his own face being reflected in a pool of water and fell in love with himself on the spot; hence narcissism means the act of admiring oneself considerably. It is natural to admire oneself, but admiring oneself excessively is abnormal and is narcissistic. Narcissistic behavior is also a manifestation of self-pride or an expression of an ego which loves itself considerably and which derives great satisfaction from observing the physical and mental beauty of the self.

49 CLASS DISTINCTION

"Human beings like to form cliques, which can be described as classes" - Anonymous

In India, as was once in China, there was and there is still a certain degree of class distinction; Brahmins, the gentry class or caste, the property-owning class, did not mingle with the lower classes; Brahmins and peasants, e.g., were not allowed to marry one another.

In view of the vast differences in individual abilities and opportunities, individuals tend to differ as to the amount of wealth they acquire; the acquisition of wealth develops into some sort of a competition or a race and those who are proud of their wealth and who do not want their poorer contemporaries to make "parasites" of themselves naturally set up a psychological barrier against such "parasites"; they do not allow members of their class to mingle with or to marry members of a lower class, or to be too friendly with them. The inevitable result is that a member of the lower class would feel the social scorn a member of the higher class held towards him. Such was the case in Ancient India, and even in Medieval England.

Today, class distinction is not so marked. But we are aware of its presence. Do we not hear of social snobs, people who continually seek the company, the friendship and the favors of wealthy people? Class distinction is a mental attitude; the mind places too great an importance on the material comforts and luxuries of life; class distinction is responsible for creating a favorable impression of the rich, the well-to-do, and an unfavorable impression of the lower classes, associating more often than not all the bad qualities, such as criminal tendency, feeble-mindedness and diseases, with them. This, of course, is not fair, for the rich do produce criminals and idiots or spread diseases. Class distinction is the result of capitalism, while in a communist or socialist state where economic enterprises are state-owned it is almost non-existent; in a capitalist society, everybody has the right to acquire as much wealth and property as possible, and some people may even deprive others of the means of survival. Therefore, to avoid class distinction, we need to change our social system, our system of government.

50 CONSERVATISM

"A conservative or old-fashioned person is like an antique"
- Anonymous

Conservatism is the state or condition of adhering rigidly to past habits and ideas; conservatism is the anti-thesis of modernism, which is the attitude of looking towards the future and being willing to make radical changes.

The conservative believes that past habits need not be changed, as long as they still bring the desirable results or satisfy the individual; the conservative is afraid of the drudgery of work that would be involved in radical changes, or of incurring greater risks. They believe that if past experience has shown that certain cultural habits are worth keeping, it is better to cling to old habits rather than adopt new life-styles, whose value has not been proven and is uncertain.

The conservative is essentially an individual who regards his ancestors with more respect than should be the case and feels thankful to them for the culture they had formed. Conservative people do not favor rapid changes but prefer to stick to the sort of life they are used to living, believing that they are so used to their sort of life that they cannot adapt if made to live another way of life. Conservatism is responsible for many of the social problems faced in India today and not so long ago; it had been the stumbling-block to China's progress; however, Mao's modernistic outlook and his arduous efforts to eradicate conservatism, such as the tearing down of temples and idols, had more or less brought China out of her problems and had been responsible for its being one of the three great powers in the world today.

51 THE DISCOURAGED PERSON

"After experiencing many failures, the discouraged person fears failure as he would the devil" - Anonymous

The mind of the discouraged person is probably unable to function with the maximum possible efficiency because of the lack or total absence of success in any undertaking, any field, such as in studies. Repeated, constant lack of success, despite faithful application and a zealous desire for success, coupled with a keen determination, undoubtedly brings about discouragement or lack of confidence in oneself or one's ability. The discouraged person has the tendency to give up an undertaking altogether, and he may finally give up.

A lazy person would not feel discouraged if he lacks success, as he knows he deserves failure as he has not tried hard enough to gain it.

Lack of success may be attributed to bad luck, if not lack of ability, or lack of confidence which is responsible for the person's inability to make the fullest possible use of his ability. This lack of confidence is the state of being discouraged, if it is the result of repeated failure in a certain undertaking, e.g., in studies. To repeat the act of trying to achieve success in the undertaking and to meet with another failure or more failures, may only bring about more discouragement, less confidence. As undertakings such as studies may be too important to give up, the person may repeat his undertakings and may be faced with greater discouragement or lack of confidence, until his discouragement is replaced by hopelessness and he gives up altogether.

52 INSTINCTS OF THE MIND

"Man, like all animals, have instincts, which are responsible for his acting in certain ways" - Anonymous

There are things, it seems, which need not be learnt, such as looking for food or love. A small child is aware of the need for food as he feels hungry and cries for food, whereby the parent would feed the hungry, crying child, after which the child would be silent. When the child grows older, it is capable of snatching or pinching the food from the kitchen, or it may clamor for food when it is hungry; this behavior is not taught, the ability to behave thus is inborn - this behavior is instinctive.

Instinctive behavior is behavior that enables the individual to satisfy a basic need and it is natural or inborn. The basic needs of the individual are food, love, shelter and security. The individual has in his mind the instincts which make him exhibit such behaviors as are necessary in order that his basic needs are satisfied. Every man was born with instincts and it is the instincts which make up the ego and bring about the egoistic feelings in the individual.

53 MIND AND LOGIC

"Though the mind is logical, it often arrives at the wrong conclusions due to prejudices" - Anonymous

Mind and logic are two inseparable things. In order that there is logic there has to be the mind. Logic is the relevant relationship between objects or between statements or premises. Logic is the result of intuition or "feeling of truth" or "awareness of truth".

Many things are logical because our intuition perceives them to be logical. If, however, others question the logic of these things, which, to us, are logical, we would start doubting their logic and would think about these things.

In order that logic exists, there has to be perception, awareness or experience. Only when there are facts or truths, or assumptions such as premises or statements, would there be logic.

54 MYSTICISM OF THE MIND

"The mind is powerful but mysterious, like a god" -
Anonymous

The mind mystifies us; it awes us with its capabilities and
potentials. Its origin is unknown. The mind may be regarded
as the soul; now and again, people have described their past
lives, and hypnosis enables a person sometimes to relate his
past lives. Is it true that when a person dies, his soul leaves
the body and takes another form, through the process of
reincarnation? It seems so. The mind is mystifying and it
distinguishes living things from non-living things. Is it true
that supposedly non-living things are really lifeless? This
again is hard to ascertain. Even living things vary and non-
living things vary more from living things.

The mind is capable of another thing, extra-sensory
perception or clairvoyance; some minds are capable of
predicting the future and are astonishing. How do we explain
extra-sensory perception? It is a rare quality of the mind -
this capability of extra-sensory perception. The mind will
continue to baffle us so.

55 THE PROPER CONDUCT FOR HAPPY LIVING

"Life is give us not to enjoy, but to overcome" -
Schopenhauer

To live happily, one needs to be agreeable to and with one's
fellow beings. It means having the same interests, the same
attitudes, the same ambitions and desires, if possible.

It may seem idealistic to stipulate what the ingredients for a
happy life are. Inevitably, success is important - success in
love, in work, in social life, constitutes a happy life. In short,
life should not be full of suffering, sorrow, misunderstanding
and quarrel. Life should be full of agreeableness, pleasure
and freedom, for man was born free, to find pleasure and to
make himself happy. Only then can life have meaning.

To live harmoniously, one should not be too selfish or too
self-centered. One should try to cultivate an outgoing
personality. One should exercise intelligence to achieve
success for oneself and should not put others at an
unnecessary disadvantage while doing so. In short avoid
sabotaging, cheating or swindling. It is very important to help
people if necessary. Do not direct all your ingenuity and
intelligence only to your own well-being, devote some to
others, your less fortunate fellow-men. The respect that
others hold towards you is very important. Surely you do not
want to live in a society in which everyone scorns you,
despises you and hates you. It is important to present an
honest, outgoing personality. To have an outgoing
personality, one needs to be rid of diffidence and lack of
initiative. Be creative in a way that entertains, exercise skills

in intellectual tasks and be happy and contented after their completion, at the same time making people respect one's intellect. But do not show off.

Always put yourself in others' shoes. Think of others and show that you think of them and have sincere concern for them. Look around at both the fortunate and the unfortunate and develop a philosophy of life which both would find agreeable. Stretch your imagination. By doing so, you would understand people and the world better and know your own position in life.

To be happy also means to be free from worries of all kinds, such as monetary worries, worries about success in life, et al. One should try to mix well with friends to enjoy and take advantage of the good things in life. Avoid bad habits at all costs, such as drug-taking, stealing and lying. Develop a healthy outlook, with both the welfare of oneself and others in mind. Exercising intelligence wisely is no easy task. Many bright people impress and gain a certain amount of success with intelligence, but they fail to use this intelligence to make others happy, probably because of personality factors. Such people may feel uneasy in the presence of friends and may even be social outcasts. Failure in romance probably has a more diffidence-causing effect than personality problems such as nervousness and lack of concentration, and, lack of success in important aspects of life such as studies and work. Pessimism is the devil of unhappiness; one should develop an outgoing, or relaxed, attitude if possible to avoid abject pessimism.

One should try one's very best to prove oneself. But do not cause others to feel stupid or incapable. Have faith in others. Always give others the benefit of a doubt, a certain degree of trust. But be cautious about trusting someone wholeheartedly to avoid being played out and being disappointed. Do not be vain or pompous. If one were clever, do not boast about it; be modest about one's ability so as not to make others feel they are inferior. Give others the feeling that they are important at least to you as friends or acquaintances.

One should avoid people who do not appreciate one's personality or one's ability so as to avoid misunderstandings or quarrels; such misunderstandings and quarrels would make one feel bitter and unhappy.

In summary, one should be conventional and not too much above the average in intellect so as to be able to understand one's fellow-men as well as to be understood by them. If one's intelligence were extremely high, there is the risk of one being accused of being ridiculous by the average person who could not understand one's ideas and arguments. One should try to be as sociable as one could be and avoid bad habits and unworthy company. To the reader, all this is probably common sense and to be expected. However, a look around us should convince us that this common sense is not so common after all, and, the reverse appears to be the case. All this here should be a wake-up call to all fellow-men.

56 WIT AND WISDOM ON MAN AND LIFE (ANONYMOUS QUOTABLE QUOTES)

1] A writer is a great writer as long as most people think they are good readers.
2] Wickedness is evil of the mind just as evil of wickedness is evil to the victim of the evil of the mind.
3] Saints do not exist, good men exist, evil men exist, and good and evil men also exist.
4] Classification is the cause of class-consciousness, and classes exist in school to favor classification.
5] I suffer fools gladly because I am happy I am not one myself and because they prove to me so - how foolish can I be to assume that fools prove me so.
6] Speed gives convenience to most and some inconvenience to others, whose cars must have been smashed up by practically racing cars.
7] Risk is possibility deemed, whilst possibility is deemed with risk.
8] The earth rotates round the sun because it is round just like the ball that rolls round and round.
9] Things that are worth quoting are things that are worth noting as they are expected to be unexpected in the quality of their truth.
10] Poverty robs the poor of happiness and the rich of their riches, and happiness as well.
11] A lie appeals to the intuition which either makes you believe or disbelieve.
12] To live is to be able to say how unlucky that person is dead.
13] If you compare yourself to fools you will be a fool, if you compare yourself to genii, you may find yourself doubly

a fool, so do what you think is best.

14] In economics, gloom is doom.

15] Man lives with the police force so that there is law and order - no fighting and no violence. But governments and countries still contradict themselves thus by resorting to fighting and war to settle their differences. They are not dissimilar to fighting fishes.

16] Uniformity is the enemy of originality, but the best friend of uniformity is foolishness.

17] History makes us feel how different men are and know why they are so, sociology makes men feel men are a unity (society) and implies universality of brotherhood and sisterhood, the contrast of the present and the past as though "past" and "present" are not contrary enough.

18] A cook is not the best judge of his food.

19] In the presence of fools, it is not foolishness which makes a fool of you, but cleverness.

20] If you have to judge a book by its cover, make sure you judge what is written on the cover.

21] Wise men tell us no black lies as foolish men do, but the white lies they tell cause them to be accused by the foolish men who tell black lies.

22] Great minds think alike, but small minds also do not differ.

23] Two countries are at war with one another because one of the presidents does not like the other.

24] Politics is legalized gangsterism.

25] The wise man aims for the truth; the fool aims past the truth.

26] Mathematics is the conveyance of truth by abstract, clever means; even the simple truth can be made abstract, hence difficult.

27] Man is so intelligent that he could make his stupidity look like intelligence.

28] Man likes happiness but he pays to go to the cinema to watch a sad movie so that he would have the pleasure or happiness of feeling sad. Strangely, man could be happy in his sadness. How confusing and contradictory.

29] Noise exists because the word "exist" exists.

30] Books are tangible ideas.

31] Invisibility is as existent as non-existence is existent only in the mind.

32] A joke appeals to a man's faculty of foolishness just as philosophy appeals to the faculty of reason; therefore, a joker is a fool and the person who laughs is another fool.

33] Beauty is the mind without which beauty exists not.

34] A man who says he is cleverer than other people think is like a poor man who says he is rich, for would a rich man admit to anybody that he is rich?

35] A genius is a person who lets his brains take advantage of him whereas a fool lets himself take as much advantage of his brains as possible, but when finding he has none feels doubly foolish.

36] Man is apparently obsessed with being the number one in all his endeavors; he tends to go for being number one in his various activities, such as: number one runner with the fastest time, number one swimmer with the fastest time, number one footballer with the most goals, number one scholar with the highest marks, number one in intelligence and capability, number one businessman with the most business assets, number one salesman with the most sales, number one politician with the most votes, number one film star with the greatest popularity and acclaim, et al., et al. How about being number one in dying, i.e., dying fastest?

37] A true lie is as true as truth.

38] A man is not judged by his actual ability but by how he can pretend to have general ability without people knowing he is pretending.

39] Truth does not lie but the truth is that people lie, to themselves sometimes, if not to others.

40] Pretense makes a man seem better but makes itself seem worse because the man would sincerely like to stop putting up the pretense, which is causing him fear.

41] Words, the air that reach our ears and affect our eardrums variedly, sometimes penetrate them and reach the heart of the mind.

42] Better be a fool happy than a wise man unhappy.

43] Social outing is not an entire waste of time, but is a waste of other people's time, if carried out haphazardly.

44] Laziness is just lack of interest; therefore, everyone is lazy at certain things.

45] A man is dead when he cannot say he is not dead.

46] A man who says he is a fool is really a fool as long as he says he is a fool and proves himself a fool.

47] Sight gives insight and insight gives sight.

48] I admire a person not because he is worth admiring but because many people admire him.

49] When life is worth living prevention is better than cure, but when life is bad prevention only brings about the sickness.

50] The dog barks not because he does not like to bite but because he is an empty vessel.

51] Death smiles upon the person who frowns upon him but laughs at the person who welcomes him for sheer folly.

52] Nothing is further from the truth than a lie about the truth.

53] A student who is brilliant is brilliant because the teacher is brilliant, as it takes some brilliance to recognize brilliance.

57 ADVICE TO READERS

"Peace of all worldly blessings is the most valuable" -
Smallridge

"To have maturity of thought and to be an intellectual" is a high sounding ideal, one may think. However, this is achievable by anyone who strives to be honest. Being matured in thought and being intelligent are very important, especially for a person performing a responsible task or leadership role or for a person who works with his brain, a scientist, lawyer or student for example.

In addition to being honest, a person has to know his strengths and weaknesses, control the emotions and let reason dominate. This is called intellectual honesty. A person has to subjugate the ego. He has to be able to face up to criticisms and learn from them.

It is hoped that the ideas presented in this book would help the reader grow intellectually, provided that he has faith in the rousing effect of subtle or clever ideas, he is prepared to view things from more angles, he is prepared to adopt a broader outlook and experience mind expansion. A quotation from Lucie McKee is appropriate here: "What would it be like to enter a day which was an immense cube of colorless, flavorless gelatin?"

www.ingramcontent.com/pod-product-compliance
Lightning Source LLC
Chambersburg PA
CBHW072104280526
45788CB00006B/2393